ORIGINAL RANCH® FAVORITES

Original Ranch® Spinach Dip

1 container (16 ounces) sour cream (2 cups)
1 box (10 ounces) frozen chopped spinach,
     thawed and squeezed dry
1 can (8 ounces) water chestnuts, rinsed, drained
     and chopped
1 packet (1 ounce) Hidden Valley® Original
     Ranch® Seasoning & Salad Dressing Mix
1 loaf round French bread
   Fresh vegetables, for dipping

Stir together sour cream, spinach, water chestnuts and
seasoning & salad dressing mix. Chill 30 minutes. Just
before serving, cut top off bread and remove center,
reserving firm bread pieces. Fill bread bowl with dip.
Cut reserved bread into cubes. Serve dip with bread
and vegetables.

Original Ranch® Spinach Dip

Original Ranch® Snack Mix

MAKES 10 CUPS

8 cups Kellogg's® Crispix® cereal
2½ cups small pretzels
2½ cups bite-size Cheddar cheese crackers (optional)
3 tablespoons vegetable oil
1 packet (1 ounce) Hidden Valley® Original Ranch® Seasoning & Salad Dressing Mix

Combine cereal, pretzels and crackers in a gallon-size Glad® Zipper Storage Bag. Pour oil over mixture. Seal bag and toss to coat. Add seasoning & salad dressing mix; seal bag and toss again until coated.

Original Ranch® Oyster Crackers

MAKES 8 CUPS

1 box (16 ounces) oyster crackers
¼ cup vegetable oil
1 packet (1 ounce) Hidden Valley® Original Ranch® Seasoning & Salad Dressing Mix

Place crackers in a gallon-size Glad® Zipper Storage Bag. Pour oil over crackers; seal bag and toss to coat. Add seasoning & salad dressing mix; seal bag and toss again until coated. Bake on ungreased baking sheet at 250°F. for 15 to 20 minutes.

Top to bottom:
Original Ranch® Snack Mix and
Original Ranch® Oyster Crackers

Ranch Drummettes

½ cup butter or margarine
¼ cup hot pepper sauce
3 tablespoons vinegar
24 chicken wing drummettes
1 packet (1 ounce) Hidden Valley® Original
    Ranch® Seasoning & Salad Dressing Mix
½ teaspoon paprika
    Additional prepared Hidden Valley® Original
    Ranch® Seasoning & Salad Dressing Mix
    Celery sticks (optional)

Melt butter and whisk together with pepper sauce and vinegar in a small bowl. Dip drummettes in butter mixture; arrange in a single layer in a large baking pan. Sprinkle with seasoning & salad dressing mix. Bake at 350°F. for 30 to 40 minutes or until juices run clear and chicken is browned. Sprinkle with paprika. Serve with additional prepared seasoning & salad dressing mix and celery sticks, if desired.

*Top to bottom: Potato Skins
(page 26) and Ranch Drummettes*

Hidden Valley® Salsa Ranch Dip

MAKES 2½ CUPS

1 container (16 ounces) sour cream (2 cups)
1 packet (1 ounce) Hidden Valley® Original Ranch® Dips Mix
½ cup thick and chunky salsa
 Chopped tomatoes and diced green chiles (optional)
 Tortilla chips, for dipping

Combine sour cream and dips mix. Stir in salsa. Add tomatoes and chiles, if desired. Chill 1 hour. Serve with tortilla chips.

Roasted Red Pepper Spread

MAKES 2 CUPS

1 cup roasted red peppers, rinsed and drained
1 package (8 ounces) cream cheese, softened
1 packet (1 ounce) Hidden Valley® Original Ranch® Seasoning & Salad Dressing Mix
 Baguette slices and sliced ripe olives (optional)

Blot dry red peppers. In a food processor fitted with a metal blade, combine peppers, cream cheese and seasoning & salad dressing mix; process until smooth. Spread on baguette slices and garnish with olives, if desired.

Hidden Valley® Salsa Ranch Dip

Ranch Chicken Pizza

MAKES 8 SERVINGS

½ cup Hidden Valley® Original Ranch® Dressing
1 package (3 ounces) cream cheese, softened
2 tablespoons tomato paste
1 cup chopped cooked chicken
1 (12-inch) prebaked pizza crust
½ cup roasted red pepper strips, rinsed and
    drained
1 can (2¼ ounces) sliced ripe olives, drained
¼ cup chopped green onions
1 cup (4 ounces) shredded mozzarella cheese

Preheat oven to 450°F. Beat dressing, cream cheese
and tomato paste until smooth. Stir in chicken; spread
mixture on pizza crust. Arrange red peppers, olives and
onions on pizza; sprinkle with mozzarella cheese. Bake
at 450°F. for 15 minutes or until hot and bubbly.

Ranch Chicken Pizza

Ranch Crispy Chicken

MAKES 4 TO 6 SERVINGS

¼ cup unseasoned dry bread crumbs or cornflake crumbs
1 packet (1 ounce) Hidden Valley® Original Ranch® Seasoning & Salad Dressing Mix
6 bone-in chicken pieces

Combine bread crumbs and seasoning & salad dressing mix in a gallon-size Glad® Zipper Storage Bag. Add chicken pieces; seal bag. Shake to coat chicken. Bake chicken on ungreased baking pan at 375°F. for 50 minutes or until no longer pink in center and juices run clear.

Savory Baked Fish

MAKES 6 SERVINGS

6 boneless fish fillets, such as scrod, flounder or other mild white fish (about 8 ounces *each*)
¾ cup Hidden Valley® Original Ranch® Dressing
Julienned vegetables, cooked (optional)

Arrange fish fillets in a large oiled baking pan. Spread each fillet with 2 tablespoons dressing. Bake at 375°F. for 10 to 20 minutes, depending on thickness of fish, or until fish flakes when tested with a fork. Finish under broiler to brown top. Serve on julienned vegetables, if desired.

Ranch Crispy Chicken

Pork Tenderloin with Red Pepper Sauce

MAKES 1 ¼ CUPS SAUCE

1 cup chopped onion
¼ cup olive oil
1 cup roasted red peppers, rinsed and drained
¾ cup sour cream
1 packet (1 ounce) Hidden Valley® Original Ranch® Seasoning & Salad Dressing Mix
2 pork tenderloins (about 1 pound each), cooked and sliced

Sauté onion in olive oil in a large skillet until soft and lightly browned. Stir in red peppers and heat through. Remove skillet from heat; stir in sour cream and seasoning & salad dressing mix. Transfer warm mixture to food processor and purée until smooth. Serve warm over sliced pork tenderloin.

SERVING SUGGESTION: This sauce is also good served over steak and chicken or used cold as a sandwich spread.

Pork Tenderloin with Red Pepper Sauce

Chicken Caesar Tetrazzini

MAKES 4 SERVINGS

8 ounces uncooked spaghetti
2 cups shredded or cubed cooked chicken
1 cup chicken broth
1 cup Hidden Valley® Caesar with Crushed Garlic
1 jar (4½ ounces) sliced mushrooms, drained
½ cup grated Parmesan cheese
2 tablespoons dry bread crumbs

Cook spaghetti according to package directions. Drain and combine with chicken, broth, dressing and mushrooms in a large mixing bowl. Place mixture in a 2-quart casserole. Mix together cheese and bread crumbs; sprinkle over spaghetti mixture. Bake at 350°F. for 25 minutes or until casserole is hot and bubbly.

Chicken Caesar Tetrazzini

Green Chile Chicken Enchiladas

  2 cups shredded cooked chicken
1½ cups (6 ounces) shredded Mexican cheese
      blend or Cheddar cheese, divided
  ½ cup Hidden Valley® Original Ranch® Dressing
  ¼ cup sour cream
  2 tablespoons canned diced green chiles, rinsed
      and drained
  4 (9- to 10-inch) flour tortillas, warmed

Mix together chicken, ¾ cup cheese, dressing, sour cream and green chiles in a medium bowl. Divide evenly down center of each tortilla. Roll up tortillas and place, seam side down, in a 9-inch baking dish. Top with remaining ¾ cup cheese. Bake at 350°F. for 20 minutes or until cheese is melted and lightly browned.

NOTE: Purchase rotisserie chicken at your favorite store to add great taste and save preparation time.

Green Chile Chicken Enchilada

Original Ranch® Roasted Potatoes

MAKES 4 TO 6 SERVINGS

2 pounds small red potatoes, quartered
¼ cup vegetable oil
1 packet (1 ounce) Hidden Valley® Original Ranch® Seasoning & Salad Dressing Mix

Place potatoes in a gallon-size Glad® Zipper Storage Bag. Pour oil over potatoes. Seal bag and toss to coat. Add seasoning & salad dressing mix; seal bag and toss again until coated. Bake in ungreased baking pan at 450°F. for 30 to 35 minutes or until potatoes are brown and crisp.

Creamy Broccoli and Cheese

MAKES 4 SERVINGS

1 package (8 ounces) cream cheese, softened
¾ cup milk
1 packet (1 ounce) Hidden Valley® Original Ranch® Seasoning & Salad Dressing Mix
1 pound fresh broccoli, cooked and drained
½ cup (2 ounces) shredded sharp Cheddar cheese

In a food processor fitted with a metal blade, blend cream cheese, milk and seasoning & salad dressing mix until smooth. Pour over broccoli in a 9-inch baking dish; stir well. Top with cheese. Bake at 350°F. for 25 minutes or until cheese is melted.

Original Ranch® Roasted Potatoes

Hidden Valley® Wraps

 1 cup Hidden Valley® Original Ranch® Dressing
 1 package (8 ounces) cream cheese, softened
10 ounces sliced turkey breast
10 ounces Monterey Jack cheese slices
 2 large avocados, peeled and thinly sliced
 2 medium tomatoes, thinly sliced
    Shredded lettuce
 4 (12-inch) flour tortillas, warmed

Beat together dressing and cream cheese. Evenly layer half the turkey, Monterey Jack cheese, dressing mixture, avocados, tomatoes and lettuce among tortillas, leaving a 1-inch border around edges. Repeat layering with remaining ingredients. Fold right and left edges of tortillas into centers over the filling. Fold the bottom edge toward the center and roll firmly until completely wrapped. Place seam side down and cut in half diagonally.

Hidden Valley® Wraps

Napa Valley Chicken Salad

MAKES 4 SERVINGS

2 cups diced cooked chicken
1 cup seedless red grapes, halved
1 cup diced celery
½ cup chopped toasted pecans
¼ cup thinly sliced green onions
½ cup Hidden Valley® Original Ranch® Dressing
1 teaspoon Dijon mustard

Combine chicken, grapes, celery, pecans and onions in a medium bowl. Stir together dressing and mustard; toss with salad. Cover and refrigerate for 2 hours.

Potato Skins

MAKES 8 TO 10 SERVINGS

4 baked potatoes, quartered
¼ cup sour cream
1 packet (1 ounce) Hidden Valley® Original Ranch® Seasoning & Salad Dressing Mix
1 cup (4 ounces) shredded Cheddar cheese Sliced green onions and/or bacon pieces★ (optional)

★*Crisp-cooked, crumbled bacon may be used.*

Scoop potato out of skins; combine potatoes with sour cream and seasoning & salad dressing mix. Fill skins with mixture. Sprinkle with cheese. Bake at 375°F. for 12 to 15 minutes or until cheese is melted. Garnish with green onions and/or bacon bits, if desired.

Napa Valley Chicken Salad

Ham Salad Bread Bowls

MAKES 4 SERVINGS (OR 3 CUPS SALAD)

- ¾ pound thick sliced deli ham
- ⅔ cup shredded Swiss cheese
- ½ cup Hidden Valley® Original Ranch® Dressing
- ¼ cup chopped green onions
- ¼ cup finely chopped sweet gherkin or dill pickles
- 4 whole Kaiser rolls (4-inch diameter)

Finely dice ham to make about 2⅓ cups; combine with cheese, dressing, onions and pickles in a medium mixing bowl. Cut a thin slice off the top of each roll. Scoop out center to within ¼ inch from edge, forming a bowl. Stuff ham salad gently into bread bowls.

Ranch Artichoke Spread

MAKES 1½ CUPS

- 1 can (14 ounces) artichoke hearts, rinsed, drained
- ¾ cup Hidden Valley® Original Ranch® Dressing
- ¼ cup sour cream
- ¼ cup grated Parmesan cheese
  Crackers or French bread slices

Coarsely chop artichokes and combine with dressing, sour cream and Parmesan cheese. Chill 30 minutes. Spread on crackers or bread slices to serve.

Ham Salad Bread Bowl

Ranch Bacon and Egg Salad Sandwich

MAKES 4 SANDWICHES (ABOUT 2 CUPS SALAD)

6 hard-cooked eggs, cooled and peeled
¼ cup Hidden Valley® Original Ranch® Dressing
¼ cup diced celery
3 tablespoons crisp-cooked, crumbled bacon★
1 tablespoon diced green onion
8 slices sandwich bread
Lettuce and tomato (optional)

★*Bacon pieces may be used.*

Coarsely chop eggs. Combine with dressing, celery, bacon and onion in a medium mixing bowl; mix well. Chill until just before serving. Spread salad evenly on 4 bread slices; arrange lettuce and tomato on egg salad, if desired. Top with remaining bread slices.

Salinas Ranch Dressing

MAKES 2 CUPS

2 cups Hidden Valley® Original Ranch® Dressing
½ cup finely chopped drained marinated
   artichoke hearts
¼ cup grated Parmesan cheese

Stir together dressing, artichoke hearts and cheese. Chill.

SERVING SUGGESTION: Serve dressing over mixed salad greens, cold cooked chicken or cold poached fish.